RE-MEMBERING

The Ministry of Welcoming Alienated and Inactive Catholics

Sarah Harmony

A Liturgical Press Book

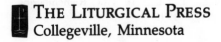

THE LITURGICAL PRESS
Collegeville, Minnesota

Cover design by Mary Jo Pauly

1   2   3   4   5   6   7   8   9

Library of Congress Cataloging-in-Publication Data

Harmony, Sarah, 1936–
    Re-membering : the ministry of welcoming alienated and inactive
Catholics / Sarah Harmony.
        p.   cm.
    ISBN 0-8146-1997-5
    1. Church work with ex-church members—Catholic Church.   2. Church
work with ex-church members—United States.   3. Catholic Church—
United States—Membership.   4. Reconciliation—Religious aspects—
Catholic Church.   I. Title.   II. Title: Remembering.
    BX2347.8.E82H37   1991   91-12962
    259—dc20   CIP

CONTENTS

FOREWORD

THE CHURCH'S PENITENTIAL DISCIPLINE, and the shape of the rite of penance, have both undergone frequent, and sometimes dramatic, change over the course of Christian history. Each of those changes, without exception, has been a response to demand from the community of believers who were discontent with the present practice.

In our own day, penitential discipline and the liturgy of penance clearly are being challenged. The crisis of penance is not so much the result of a loss of a sense of sin. People are no less good or bad today than they were in any other period of human history. There is confusion, however, about how to define sin in a day far more aware of "systems" theory, ecological, psychological, and sociological determinants to behavior, and the like. We are all deeply involved in a world gone awry; partly because we have chosen our alienations, partly because we are caught up in the swirl of the dark side of our times. There is need for a holistic response to the people's call for forgiveness, healing, and liberation.

All this is true, perhaps even especially so, for those who have not been actively participating in the struggles of the believing community. Some simply drifted away; others left because of sirens of the false gods of our day; some were locked out by a less than caring church community or leadership. And while they have been experiencing the same challenges to belief, fidelity, authenticity, and integrity as their church-going friends, inactives have not had the same opportunities for pastoral care, biblical challenge, liturgical inspiration, and communal involvement in moral decision making as have those who remained actively involved in church life. Inactive Catholics deserve particular care, nurturing, support, and challenge when their lives lead them to begin to question their "outsider" posture. Sifting and sorting through the basic matter of their separation from church life, they need the chance to hear the gospel call to conversion, no less or more than do the ones who never walked away. We all are on a journey of conversion/reconciliation.

In recent years many parish catechumenate directors have told the training teams of the North American Forum on the Catechumenate that Catholics who have been estranged from the Church have sought out the catechumenate as a vehicle for their exploration of the question of return to active life in the community. Sometimes the catechumenate has been an appropriate place for them to examine that question, and adaptations of catechumenate ministry have met that need. More often, however, because of the special needs of each group, it has been recognized that two different kinds of gathering are in order. In 1986 the Forum gathered pastoral ministers who had been experimenting with a restored order of penitents, fashioned under different titles, to explore the possibility of their sharing the best of their experience. That led to the establishment of Forum's Re-Membering Church workshop. In over thirty of these workshops throughout the U.S., Canada, England, Ireland, Australia, and New Zealand, participants have been led through a process meant to introduce them to the dynamics of ministry among people who have been estranged from the Church.

The parish program described in this manual is one enfleshment of the principles espoused in that workshop, authored by a regular team member of that Forum training event. The Re-Membering Community at Blessed Sacrament Parish, like those in virtually hundreds of parishes in other parts of the U.S., Canada, and overseas, may well be one of those approaches to liturgical reform which marks the history of penance. Like every other reform of penance, it is the work of a people seeking to respond to the needs of a particular time and place. Clearly in line with some of the earliest manifestations of the Church's ancient tradition, it also constitutes a response to the challenge for the renewal of penance begun in the Second Vatican Council and echoed in the 1983 Synod of Bishops in Rome. At that synod, in fact, Joseph Cardinal Bernardin specifically called for such a pastoral response as exemplified in Blessed Sacrament's Re-Membering Community.

If the liturgy and discipline of penance are under challenge today, then it is efforts like the Re-Membering Community which may well constitute our best hope at responding. It is a process true to the tradition, liturgically well-founded, pastorally sensitive, and open to the guidance of the Spirit working in ordinary lives. That is no small matter.

James Lopresti
November 30, 1989

PREFACE

THE RE-MEMBERING COMMUNITY of my home parish is involved in the ministry of reconciliation. Its specific purpose is to provide a warm welcoming place that aids alienated and inactive Catholics in their return to the table of the Lord and to an active Catholic life as disciples of Jesus Christ.

Within this community we have come to realize that this return is not an instant thing. Coming home—to self, to community, to God—is a conversion process that requires time. It takes time to uncover the broken areas of lives that are in need of healing, liberation, and forgiveness; time to begin this healing; time for Christian companionship to grow; time to ask questions; time for discernment; time for re-conversion to happen within the heart of the returning Catholic and within the heart of the community welcoming the returning Catholic.

While this is by no means the only way people return to the Church in our parish, it is proving to be the most effective and permanent way. Re-membering results in renewed Catholics who become active in their faith. The sacrament of penance experienced in our re-membering community is one of several options available in our parish. We celebrate individual penance on a weekly basis and we also have seasonal celebrations of communal penance, but we are finding that penance experienced during the six weeks of Lent has greatly benefited the prayer life of many and has proved almost invaluable to those returning to the Church.

Several years ago, with the help of our pastor, we formed a team to spend time with returning Catholics. The original team consisted of myself as parish staff co-ordinator along with Joan, a co-ordinator from the parish community, and one of our parish priests, Steve. Other original team members were Agnes, Mary Ann, Bill, Norma, Gene, and Mike our liturgist. Working with us was Fr. James Lopresti of the North American Forum on the Catechumenate. Jim (Father Lopresti) was a regular team member and advisor and he brought to us his work on and vision of penance and reconciliation. This team has since changed and enlarged, but our parish will always be grateful to these people who took the dream and through many long and hard struggles put flesh on the dream; who took the time to recognize their own need for healing, liberation, and forgiveness; who took the time to nurture conversion in themselves and in others; who took the time to discover what it means to be church for one another.

That team learned the real truths of this ministry from their experiences with the penitents and companions, especially those who were part of our first order of penitents. It was from Agnes who was companion to penitent Eileen, from Kevin who was companion to penitent Tom, from Sandy who was companion to penitent Pat, and from Lisa who was companion to penitent Stephanie that we were able to take all our dreams, ideas, hopes, and the time that was invested and put them into the real ministry of re-membering.

We named ourselves the Re-Membering Community but we came to realize that the word re-member or remember means more than merely re-joining. It means to recall, to keep in mind, or to bring into reality. In the ancient scriptural sense it means to actually bring a person, thought, or event into the present time. This ministry means to re-member alienated Catholics but it also means that these alienated and inactive Catholics are again remembering their baptismal heritage. Our community remembers in prayer the wounds and healings, the captivities and liberations, the guilts and the forgivenesses of all those who have shared our journey with us. For it has been in sharing our lives with one another that we have learned to remember while re-membering.

In writing this book I have sought to remember our experiences in forming our re-membering community. This book is dedicated to that original forming team. I will also use the experiences of other communities that I have helped establish and other communities who have shared their birthing process with me. This book is written so that other parish communities may begin their own ministry of reconciliation in remembering and re-membering.

Duck, North Carolina
Springfield, Virginia

1

THE MINISTRY
Values and Principles

Behold I am making all things new, don't you feel it?
Isaiah

JESUS CHRIST IS THE SACRAMENT OF RECONCILIATION; therefore, reconciling all things to God is the mission of the body of Christ, the Church community. The specific ministry of reconciling or re-membering the community's alienated flows from this mission of the Church and is carried out by and through parish communities. A parish's re-membering ministry, then, is among the inactive and alienated of the Catholic Church as they consider a return to an active faith life.[1]

The re-membering ministry seeks to help discover within the lives of inactive and alienated Catholics those areas that are broken or wounded and in need of healing, that are bound or held captive and in need of liberating, that are guilt ridden and in need of forgiving. This ministry leads its ministers into recognizing those areas of their own lives that are in need of healing, liberation, or forgiveness. It also realizes that the penitential pil-

---

[1]In this work we will use both the word re-membering and the word remembering since both are important to this ministry. Re-membering here means to join again, while the word remembering has a fuller meaning. It means to recall to mind, but it also bears the scriptural sense of actually bringing a person or event into the present.

grimage is a lifelong process and it honors the time that is required for this process of conversion. The ministry of re-membering is rooted in Christian companionship, rejoices in the loving mercy of God, and celebrates reconciliation. Indeed, remembering and reconciling is a ministry that encompasses and belongs to all of the Church community. Those people involved in the re-membering ministry know that they are ministering ''among'' and not ''to'' the alienated.

It is only when the entire baptized community recognizes its own woundedness and need for healing that it becomes an effective and compassionate healer for those Catholics who, for a variety of reasons, feel alienated from the Church. These alienated Catholics usually became physically inactive when they distanced themselves from active participation in the liturgical life of the Church, but in some cases they became emotionally or spiritually distanced from the Church while still worshiping with the community.

A parish's re-membering community usually works with those Catholics whose alienations have caused them to leave the active liturgical life of the Church. These people have been labeled ''fallen-away,'' ''lapsed,'' or ''former,'' but such titles become inappropriate once the faith stories of these people are told. Those involved in the ministry of re-membering have learned that Catholics leave an active participation in the Church for many reasons. James Lopresti, in his booklet *Penance: A Reform Proposal for the Rite,* identifies the types of alienation that lead to a separation from the Church.[2] Some people are ''unawakened.'' They have never fully known Jesus Christ nor have they fully connected with the Catholic Church: they have not heard the gospel. Some are ''prophetically'' alienated. They have some claim, true or false, against the Church community: they feel that the Church community is not faithful to the demands

[2]James Lopresti, *Penance: A Reform Proposal for the Rite* (Washington: The Pastoral Press, 1987) 8–10.

of the gospel. Many are "truly" alienated. They have heard the gospel and have rejected it. But most people are a combination of all three types of alienation.

The unawakened are usually found in the parish catechumenate. There they are uninitiated people with little knowledge of the gospel. But the unawakened also come to the re-membering community. There they are usually adults who were fully initiated at a young age but who have very little knowledge of the gospel message. Some unawakened left the Church when their parents became inactive. Some remained nominally in the Church, but only have an inherited, unawakened faith. Most unawakened simply never developed an adult faith. The one thing that all unawakened people share is the fact that they have not adequately or fully heard the gospel. Those involved in the re-membering ministry will tell and listen to faith stories as they share the gospel and its values with the unawakened. They will answer questions that are asked and guide where guidance is necessary. They will be Christian companions during the awakening and conversion.

The prophetically alienated come to the re-membering community with claims that the Church community itself is not acting according to the gospel. Many women today have a prophetic claim against the Church; so do many gays and also racial and cultural minority groups. The rules and regulations governing the lifestyles of our ordained clergy is another area of possible prophetic alienation. The important issue in a prophetic alienation is that the alienated person *feels* an injustice from the Church community. It is not important whether their claim is valid, nor is it important whether anyone agrees with their claim. Those in the re-membering ministry will listen to the stories of these prophetically alienated Catholics, will catechize where misinformation is present, and will dialogue with them in the hope that the dialogue will lead to the beginning of a mutual healing between the Church community and the prophetically alienated.

The truly alienated come to the re-membering community with a multitude of hurts and pains from sin; with things they have done and things they should have done. They need to be met by a loving and compassionate Church, represented in the re-membering community, who will take the time to sit and to listen, to share faith stories, to inform, to be a Christian companion while re-conversions are taking place, and then to celebrate ritually this re-connectedness.

Again, recall that most people have a bit of all three types of alienation and require most of the care listed above. They should be welcomed with great hospitality, listened to carefully, given the gospel message both in Scripture and in the personal witness of team members. Their questions need to be answered and prayer, both personal and communal, is essential. Re-membering Catholics need the parish community, the re-membering community, and a special spiritual friend called a companion. This service among the inactive and alienated can truly make us a re-membering and a remembering Church.

Ministering among these re-membering Catholics is often intense, usually exciting, always heartfilled, occasionally discouraging, surprisingly joyful, and constantly challenging. This ministry calls its ministers to complete involvement in the lives of those for whom they are caring. Participation in this ministry means working on the fringes of the Church. It means listening with compassion and loving with Christ-like passion. It means getting in touch with personal brokenness. It means being church for one another.

One of the most important expressions of being church for one another is companionship. *Webster's Dictionary* calls a companion a bread or meal fellow and one who travels with another. It is easy to see why companionship is necessary in every reconciling relationship. It forms the heart of the re-membering ministry. In the re-membering ministry, companionship that was modeled in the parish community will begin within the team itself and grow to include the re-membering Catholics. A re-membering Catholic who has been alienated and away from the active life of the Church must feel the warmth and the welcome of Christian companionship before the journey of reconciliation can begin.

Christian companionship is illustrated beautifully in Scripture, and this gospel value is witnessed today in different areas of our society. Most twelve-step programs encompass companioned relationships. Christian initiation of adults depends heavily on the companionship of sponsors, and in the same manner the faith companions of the re-membering Catholics are an integral part of the penitential journey of return. Ideally, the two people involved in a companioned relationship will build deep levels of faith and trust in each other through the sharing of their faith stories, Scripture, and prayer. In the re-membering ministry companionship is considered sacred ground because it is in true faith sharing that re-membering Catholics and team alike often meet Jesus again and begin their reconciliation.

The paths of reconciliation are as diverse as the paths of alienation, and some people are never able to complete their reconciliation. But for each re-membering Catholic who moves toward reconciliation there are several things to consider. Each of these re-membering Catholics requires a different amount of time to discover the roots of their alienations and still more time for their process of conversion that leads to healing, liberation, and forgiveness. Each one must come to terms with those situations that have led to their separation from the Church community. They need to make adult decisions concerning their faith lives. Most important of all they have to discover the welcoming mercy of God that meets us lovingly in our most vulnerable places of sin.

When a re-membering Catholic has spent some time in the process of healing, liberation, and forgiveness, has experienced re-conversion to Jesus, and is ready again to make a commitment to the gospel, then they are ready to celebrate their return ritually. The fullest expression of this celebration of return is in the renewed order of penitents.[3]

In the renewed order of penitents, a re-membering Catholic is initiated into the order on Ash Wednesday with the sign of the ash. Along with the rest of the parish community, but in a special way, they bear the honorable name of penitent. During Lent they spend time in prayer and meditation, with Sunday and daily Scriptures, in conversations with their companion. They will probably seek the wisdom of a spiritual guide and confessor. Their penitential journey is incorporated into the prayer of the whole Church community. They celebrate a process of sacramental penance and reconciliation beginning with the confession of God's mercy on Ash Wednesday and culminating with public absolution on Holy Thursday. And finally, they joyfully celebrate their return to the Eucharistic table with the parish community on Holy Thursday. During the Easter season they join the entire Church community in discernment of mission and ministry as they prepare for Pentecost.

Sometimes a re-membering Catholic chooses to celebrate their return ritually in the midst of the Church community with a selected confessor during a parish communal celebration of penance. Since the prayer of the community is another important key in the re-membering ministry, there should always be some kind of a community celebration of return for all re-membering Catholics.

To be a companion or a minister among the re-membering of our Catholic community is a sacred privilege. To minister among the alienated is to welcome, to listen, to share stories,

[3]Some parishes working with alienated Catholics call the entire process of re-membering the order of penitents. For this manual we will refer to the Re-Membering Community as that time that inactive and alienated Catholics spend in discernment and preparation for return to the table and an active faith life. The order of penitents will be that final stage during Lent when a re-membering Catholic becomes a penitent and prepares in an intense way for their return to the table of apostles and witnesses on Holy Thursday.

to pray, to celebrate, to love, and to provide a fertile ground for the seeds of conversion. When this has happened, then reconciliation can be celebrated in the joyful return of a fully re-membered and re-converted Catholic to the Eucharistic table of the Lord. This re-membered Catholic will then go forth from that table as an active apostle and witness for Jesus Christ.

Summary

Jesus Christ is our sacrament of reconciliation and we, the body of Christ, are called to carry out his reconciling mission. The ministry of re-membering the Church's alienated and inactive flows from this reconciling mission of the whole Church.

A parish's re-membering community represents the whole Church as they seek to bring healing, liberation, and forgive-ness to those who are unawakened, truly, or prophetically alien-ated. This pilgrimage of reconciliation is indeed a lifetime jour-ney, and if a re-membering community is to carry out the Church's mission, then each individual member, along with the Church community itself, must be in touch with their peniten-tial journey. When conversion, repentance, and reconciliation have begun, then the body of Christ, the Church, can authenti-cally gather around the table of apostles and witnesses.

2

THE TEAM
Membership and Formation

Out of love, place yourselves at one another's service. . . .
You shall love your neighbor as yourself.   Gal 5:12

THE JOYFUL NEWS OF THE GOSPEL is that Jesus Christ welcomes back all sinners who repent and return to him. When a parish community recognizes that reconciliation is the mission of the entire Church community, and when they embrace this ministry of reconciliation, then they are ready to begin the work of a re-membering community. For a re-membering community to flourish well in a parish, that parish will need to have the fertile ground of a well-established, loving, and caring community that has firm roots in Christian initiation. From the beginning it is necessary to see penance and reconciliation as a lifelong process of conversion. James Dallen, in his book *The Reconciling Community,* explains that the process of conversion is the key to the sacrament of penance.[1] Parishes should come to understand that it is essential to take this process time with potential re-membering Catholics. This time is necessary for conversions that will lead to healing, liberation, and forgiveness. To facilitate this, a parish should have a team of parishioners who are willing to journey with re-membering Catholics on their paths

[1]James Dallen, *The Reconciling Community: The Rite of Penance* (New York: Pueblo Publishing Company, 1986) 254.

of reconciliation. This special group of ministers of reconciliation is called a re-membering community team.

Selecting a Re-Membering Community Team

Personal Qualities of a Team Member

The task of selecting a re-membering community team will probably fall initially to those involved in parish leadership. In this search for parishioners who will make good team members, there are several personal qualities that are valuable to seek. A re-membering community team will benefit from people who have some or most of the following qualities:

1. *Prayerful and Faith-Filled.* The most important quality that a team member can have is to be a prayerful person of faith. A faith-filled team member will constantly work on their own penitential journey as they move closer to God. They will be familiar with the personal conversions that happen often in a Christian life. They will be open to the Spirit in their lives.

2. *Faith Sharing Abilities.* A team member should be able to share their own personal faith with the rest of the community. They should be comfortable giving witness to the importance of the gospel messages in their lives. They need a real zeal for telling their own faith story.

3. *Gentleness/Non-Judgmental.* To be a good team member a person needs to be gentle by nature. They should listen with compassion and without passing judgment, and they should have the ability to deal with other people's feelings of alienation. They must express care without evaluating. One thing that is death to the re-membering ministry is a "we, holy ones—them, sinners" mentality. A good team member will know that mercy and love come from God and that we, as his ministers, must act in the same way.

4. *Confidentiality.* Many things will be discussed and revealed in a re-membering community that require the utmost confiden-

tiality. All community members must realize that the thoughts and feelings that are shared in the re-membering ministry are never repeated outside the re-membering community. Team members must keep to themselves what is discussed within the community.

5. *Humor and Joy of Life.* Another valuable asset for a team member to have is a sense of humor and a joyful way of living life. In the re-membering community a team often deals with deep wounds and alienations. A light touch can relax a tense moment; a positive attitude can put many things into perspective.

6. *Hospitality.* To be able to make a person feel at home and welcome, to make a potential re-membering Catholic feel like they have been missed in their church family, to make a tense person feel glad that they came, and to be able to recognize giftedness in newly re-membering people are all happy gifts. Team members with these gifts make the re-membering community a comfortable place where sharing and trust can begin and where the seeds of reconciliation can be planted.

7. *Community Builders.* The re-membering community is a group of people working on their alienations and sharing the stories of their faith journeys of reconciliation. They are a group of people whose lives intersect. Parishioners who have the ability to build up this community, to make individuals into a cohesive group, and to build relationships between people are valuable members of the re-membering community team.

8. *Team Players.* The re-membering community is led by a team with certain gifts and talents among themselves. No one individual on the team will possess all the charisms necessary for the success of the whole. To belong to a re-membering team a parishioner needs to be comfortable being part of a team. They should not need to be the center of attention or feel that they alone can accomplish the task of the re-membering ministry; nor should they be so shy that they are unable to share themselves with others. Team players must be comfortable sharing their gifts and receiving the gifts of others.

Initial Team Selection

The initial selection of a re-membering community team will begin with the leader(s) or co-ordinator(s). This selection is usually done by the parish leadership. Ideally, one leader is selected from the parish leadership and one is selected from the parish family at large. This dual leadership enables a true sharing of the labors and vision between parish leadership and the entire parish family. Since initially much responsibility falls upon the leader(s) of a re-membering community, great care should be given in selecting them. Leaders will need the previously described personal qualities, but they also will need the time, patience, and perseverance that it takes to form the recruited team members into a true reconciling community.[2]

After the leader(s) have been selected they, along with the parish leadership, should go through the names of parishioners to find people who have the personal qualities and who could fill the ministry roles of companion, catechist, scripture sharer, spiritual guide, evangelists, and social and justice leaders. *(See Chapter 3 for a description of these ministry roles.)* In large parishes this can be accomplished by going through parish files. In these larger parishes there certainly will be enough people to fill the needs of a re-membering team, but the problem may be to find the right person for the right ministry role. In smaller communities knowing the parishioners and their gifts is easy, but the task of filling all the ministry roles may be more difficult. Filling all these ministry roles is the ideal to work toward, and while they are working toward this goal communities should begin their work as soon as the key ministry roles are filled. The most important ministry roles to begin with are leader(s), parish priest, scripture sharer, and catechist. Bear in mind that sometimes one person can fill more than one ministry role. Hospitality people and evangelizers may be identified from within the team.

---

[2]Smaller parishes may want to band together with a neighboring parish to form a re-membering community.

Companions can be recruited as the team forms. Social justice leaders may be added as they are found.

In searching for team members it is a good idea to recruit more people than you think you will actually need since some parishioners that are invited may be unable to serve on the team. The actual number of team members will vary according to the size of the parish and according to the number of re-membering Catholics that a re-membering community is serving. A beginning team will consist of a leader(s) and at least two other people. Some teams have grown to as many as fifteen members.

When selecting team members a balance should be maintained. There should be men and women of varying ages. Clergy, religious, and laity, married and single need to be included. There ought to be people that are representative of the average parishioner in age, education, and life style. The most valuable person to find for a re-membering team is someone who has been away from the Church and has returned. The experiences of these re-membered team members are a great asset to the entire team.

A re-membering team should include others as advisors. These advisors could be parishioners or diocesan or regional professionals. A most important advisor is someone with a background in counseling. Many times an inactive or alienated Catholic has personal or psychological problems to deal with before they can begin the re-membering process. Since this is most certainly beyond the scope of a re-membering community, the team will need help in identifying and referring these people. Also, people with experience in the Christian initiation (Rite of Christian Initiation for Adults, or RCIA) process are most beneficial to a re-membering team since the two processes are similar. If a parish has a firmly established process of Christian initiation, then members of that team have much to share with a re-membering team. Since the team will be composed of average parishioners it might also be helpful to know someone with a background in theology. When questions arise in discussion sessions, the team will benefit from having a person—in addition to other references—that they can turn to for some advice. Finally, it is important to have a liturgist working with the team. When the time comes for the ritual and sacramental celebration of the return of the re-membering Catholic, a person trained in liturgy who can work creatively will be important.

When the re-membering team leader(s) and the parish leadership have selected the appropriate parishioners for the re-membering community, then an invitation should be extended to these people to attend an informational meeting. At this meeting the re-membering ministry is discussed and any questions answered. It is important for potential team members to know just what is being asked of them as part of a re-membering team.

Many re-membering communities have found that it is important to be very specific with the requirements for a team member, but other communities have found that getting a parishioner involved in the team and then letting the commitment grow is the better approach. In either case, one of the ways to prevent team burnout is to work toward identifying a specific time commitment for team members. One suggestion for finalizing that commitment is to have a regular yearly commitment celebration of old and new team members around Pentecost. The commitment of a team member should be for a specific number of hours per week or month. This specific commitment also allows the leader(s) of a re-membering team to be able to rely on the presence and support of the team.

Once an initial team has been chosen and that team has made a commitment to the re-membering ministry, it is time to begin work among inactive and alienated Catholics. As a parish becomes involved in this ministry of reconciliation it will become obvious that service among these re-membering Catholics must be constant and continuing. Once begun, a re-membering community should always be part of the parish ministry.

During the years as team members move on to other locations or ministries it will be necessary to replace them, and as the community grows it will be important to add new team members. A re-membering team needs to plan for the ongoing recruitment of new team members.

On-Going Team Selection

New team members are necessary for all re-membering communities; therefore, teams need to develop a system for recruiting these new members. In smaller and/or stable parishes this recruitment is simple. In larger or more transitional parishes this recruitment has to be well developed. In all cases several principles apply.

First of all, as a re-membering team recruits new team members they should always go back to their original qualifications for team members. As a team forms they will be able to see more clearly just what type of person their re-membering community needs and they will be able to tell precisely what ministry roles need to be filled. Since each re-membering community is slightly different and has a personality of its own, the needs of each community will vary and these needs will also change and develop as the community matures. Good leaders must be sensitive to the special needs of their particular team.

Some of the best "new" team members may be people that have already been part of the re-membering community in some other capacity. These are people that are already familiar with the re-membering ministry. For instance, a companion from one year might become a good catechist or presenter the following year. A social planner from one year might be ready to share scripture the next year. New leaders are almost always chosen from within the existing team since it is vital for them to have a knowledge and vision of the ministry of re-membering.

As a re-membering community grows, the role of companion is ideally filled by people who have come through the re-membering process and who have been penitents during a Lenten journey in the renewed order of penitents. These people who have walked the reconciliation path make excellent guides for new re-membering Catholics.

Because this ministry is responsible for much personal faith-growth and conversion in team members, teams may tend to remain fairly stable. Usually, people committed to the re-membering ministry as team members stay with that ministry unless something special prompts them to leave. This means that the team's ongoing recruitment is not normally a difficult task.

In smaller and/or more stable parishes teams may remain intact for several years. Here the responsibility of a leader is to add new members and new ideas. This is best accomplished by recruiting to companionship and eventually to the team those people who have been former penitents.

In large and/or more transitional parishes a conscious effort needs to be made to find new team members. In this case leaders, with the assistance of the whole team, have to be constantly looking through the parish for people to be involved in the re-membering ministry.

As the ministry grows and more people learn about and begin to consider the re-membering process as a way of returning to the Church, most teams will have to seek some new members. Since a parish will be looking for re-membering team members with specific qualifications, there is seldom a general or open recruitment. Most likely those involved in the re-membering ministry will recruit new team members by personal invitation. Another helpful idea is to invite prospective new members to participate in a general way in the re-membering community for several months before a commitment is discussed. This helps both the team and the prospective new team member to select the appropriate ministry role.

As a re-membering community is born, grows, and matures it is always important to be conscious of the formation of that group of individuals into a close reconciling community.

Formation of a Re-Membering Community Team

It is the responsibility of the re-membering team leader(s) to take a group of individual people who have the gifts and talents for the re-membering ministry and to create with this group a sense of belonging and shared ministry. While it is absolutely essential to form community with re-membering ministers initially, it will be equally important to keep formation occurring as the team grows, changes, and adds new members.

A team in the re-membering ministry must articulate a shared vision of goals and objectives. This team will need to tell personal faith stories, to share scripture, to break bread together, and to become like family in their care for one another. While they truly become a community, they must also remain open to new members. This constant forming of a re-membering community team is accomplished by praying, playing, and preparing together.

Praying Together

SCRIPTURE SHARING

From the very first meeting of a fledgling re-membering community it is important for team members to tell their personal faith stories and to share Scripture. Most groups find that it is advisable to stay with the Sunday lectionary readings as they learn about, celebrate, and become part of the liturgical year. Another way of selecting Scripture is to select a passage of Scripture that speaks of the subject currently being discussed. This can easily be done by using a Bible concordance.

Initially one team member should be asked to prepare the Scriptures. This person usually is someone who shows a natural ability for faith sharing. This Scripture leader reads aloud one of the three Sunday readings (usually the gospel) or another pertinent selection and shares with the rest of the team the personal meaning of these Scriptures in their life. The team should be encouraged to respond. As time goes on and trust is built up among the team members, this sharing will deepen and more members of the team will become comfortable being the leader of Scripture.

Generally after a re-membering community is established, every discussion session or team meeting will begin with Scripture sharing since this sharing of gospel values is one of the foundation stones in the re-membering ministry.

PERSONAL AND COMMUNITY PRAYER

Daily prayer is obviously part of the life of a team member, but the expressions of prayer vary according to the personality of the individual. Many team members may also seek the counseling of spiritual advisors or guides, especially during Lent.

It often happens that several team members begin to join one another on a daily basis for prayer. Many teams have found that re-membering communities sit and pray together at Sunday and daily Mass or gather several times a week for group prayer. While this is usually not planned it seems to be a natural thing for teams to do.

Other types of community prayer are valuable when the re-membering community gathers. It is essential to include the prayer of Jesus, the Our Father. Intercessory prayer is another essential part of a re-membering community and as the lives of community members intertwine it becomes normal to pray for one another and for the needs of the community. More advanced prayer forms are reserved for team gatherings and the order of penitents.

Sometimes teams will ritualize special moments such as a commitment service at Pentecost time or a time for celebrating companionship. The sacramental celebration of penance with a selected confessor is part of the prayer life of a re-membering community team member.

RETREATS

After several organizational meetings, a re-membering community team will be ready for some quiet prayer time in a day of recollection or a retreat. These retreats should occur several times a year for an established team and they may be an organized retreat or simple days of prayer that are planned by members of the re-membering team itself.

The idea of ministering among alienated Catholics has been discussed. As they begin to work among alienated and inactive Catholics, team members naturally begin to deal with their own personal alienations and their own need for healing, liberation, and forgiveness. Scripture sharing sessions that help re-membering Catholics get in touch with their need for reconciliation also help team members discover their paths of reconciliation. This is a very beautiful and natural happening as a team discovers the truth to the words that we are *all* forgiven sinners. This is what is often called "the blur," since it is sometimes hard to distinguish between the penitential journeys of team members and those of re-membering Catholics. This does mean, however, that team members must take time aside from the work of the re-membering ministry and pay attention to their own penitential journeys. James Dunning of the North American Forum on the Catechumenate always cautions people involved in the initiating and reconciling ministries, "Thou shalt not do unto others what thou is not doing (or has done) to thyself." A re-membering community team must truly practice what they preach.

It is during this self discernment process that a retreat is valuable. Most re-membering communities have found that if a team does not take some time for themselves and their personal journeys of reconciliation, they become less effective as ministers of reconciliation. Retreats of many types are available in all parishes and dioceses. It is valuable for a team to maintain a list of available retreats in their area.

One special type of retreat for a re-membering team is called the Lenten journey. This journey is similar to the journey of re-membering Catholics as penitents in the renewed order of penitents. This retreat lasts for the season of Lent and involves the Church's ancient signs of penance: prayer, fasting, and alms-giving. It also incorporates community service, Scripture shar-ing, and meditation. It is usually led by the parish priest or a team leader. The sacramental celebration of penance, which is often experienced over this entire Lenten season, is included. Spiritual advisors are made available to team members. It is help-ful for a team to celebrate Lent in this manner before their re-membering community celebrates their first order of penitents. This enables team members to experience themselves what they have planned for the re-membering Catholic.

Playing Together

Hospitality or welcoming ministry begins with the first gather-ing of a re-membering community team and continues and grows as the community grows. If a team, and eventually re-membering Catholics, are to build up deep levels of trust that enable them to share their faith, they will have to get to know one another on a personal level. They need to become friends before they can be comfortable dealing with painful levels of hurt and al-ienation. Many re-membering communities have also discov-ered that social activities are another way for inactive Catholics to enter a re-membering community.

As a re-membering community grows they will enjoy add-ing more social activities. Team members and re-membering Catholics will become friends over pot-lucks, picnics, outings to local theaters, or sports activities.

The coffee pot should always be on any time the re-membering community gathers and time should be made for friendly conversation and for simple togetherness.

Preparing Together

Besides getting to know one another and praying together, a re-membering community team will have to take some time for educational preparations. This is important not only in the beginning but also as a team grows and matures.

Preparation and education can be done in a variety of ways. There should always be books available for individual team members to borrow or buy. Professionals can be brought in to speak to the team. One member of the team can do research on a specific subject and then report to the whole team or the whole team can spend time together working on a specific skill. It is important to follow any of these learning methods with a team discussion so that the information can be processed.

BOOKS

There are books that are necessary for team members to have available so that they may read them either as individuals or a whole team. Some of the reference books that are valuable in the re-membering ministry are listed in appendixes B and C.

SKILLS

There are some skills that are necessary for a re-membering team to have. Team members will discover that expertise in these skills will make a smoothly functioning team and community.

Listening is probably the most valuable skill and beautiful gift that team members can learn or nurture. To be a good team member in a re-membering community a person must be able to listen to themselves, to their companion, to the rest of the re-membering community, to the parish, and even to the world. Effective and active listening that does not pass judgment or try to "fix-up" is essential in the re-membering ministry.

Adult Moral Decision Making is another skill that all team members will have to develop. Re-membering Catholics usually need to become adult Catholics who are responsible for their own faith. Before a team member can lead others, they themselves must be comfortable making decisions about their faith. Sessions on adult decision making facilitate growth in faith, and should be a regular part of the re-membering community's activities for team and re-membering Catholics alike.

Communication is always an important skill as long as people and their relationships are an integral part of a process. In the re-membering process the people and their relationships are an important reason for the existence of the community; therefore, the ability to express one's self and to transmit ideas clearly is important to all team members. Effective evangelization begins with good communication skills.

Communication skills are needed for making the parish community aware of the ministry of re-membering. Since the word "re-membering" and this particular way of welcoming back inactive and alienated Catholics is relatively new to the Church, it is necessary for a re-membering team to communicate the message of the re-membering ministry to the whole parish. The methods of communication will vary from parish to parish. Probably the most effective way for a parish to become aware of the reconciling mission of the whole parish and the re-membering community is through public liturgical celebrations of return. Some other suggestions for enlightening a parish are to use the Sunday bulletin often, to have the parish priest who is part of the re-membering team speak of this ministry in his homilies and when he is working with other groups, to use local news media, to inform all parish organizations of the ministry of re-membering, or to have informational coffees after all the Masses. Once a parish community is aware of the re-membering ministry they will be able to become the neighborhood evangelizers that the re-membering community needs.

A team will also use methods and skills of communication in locating potential re-membering Catholics. Many of the methods of communicating with a parish at large will also reach potential re-membering Catholics. A team should especially search in areas of church ministry where potential re-membering Catholics are often found. Surveys by Dean Hoge tell us that over half of our returnees come back because of family life situations.[3] The parents of children receiving sacraments is therefore a natural place to start. Potential re-membering Catholics can be found in a children's catechumenate, in an infant baptismal preparation program, in classes preparing children and youth for Eucharist and confirmation. They are also found in marriage preparation programs and in support groups for the separated, divorced, and remarried.

Internal communication within the re-membering community is another important area. It is essential to the process of reconciliation for individual community members to be able to express themselves accurately to one another.

Team Meetings

In the beginning, a newly formed re-membering team will meet often. As this team grows and matures, team meetings should continue on a regular basis. This continued contact with one another provides the opportunity to plan and to organize, and it will contribute to the smooth functioning of a re-membering community.

In the beginning, teams meet anywhere from once a week to once every several weeks. It is necessary to meet often as the community gets organized and makes plans for the first and subsequent meetings and ritual celebrations.

As a re-membering community becomes established, the tendency is to hold regular meetings less often. It may become necessary, however, for the team to hold small or short meetings (thirty minutes) more often. These short meetings give the team the opportunity to keep abreast of the current needs and progress of the re-membering Catholics with whom they are working. This combination of both regular long meetings and short focused meetings seems to work well.

In an established re-membering community, the team may want to hold its regular meetings once in every season or about

[3]Dean R. Hoge, *Converts, Dropouts, Returnees* (New York: The Pilgrim Press, 1981) 139.

four times a year. These meetings will probably last several hours and offer the team the opportunity to plan for the upcoming season, to discuss the re-membering Catholics, to plan evangelization. The shorter meetings may be held at either the beginning or the end of a re-membering community discussion session, or at some other time when the team is already gathered.

In addition to the meetings of the whole team, a re-membering community may find that some smaller specialized groups will want to gather. One such group might be the companions.

The Maturing Team

One of the first signs that a re-membering community has begun to grow and change will be the increase in the number of potential re-membering Catholics coming to the community sessions. As the number of people increases, the number of team members needs to increase. This increase in numbers coupled with a deeper understanding of the re-membering ministry shows a maturing re-membering community.

Specialized Ministry

As a team grows and matures, the organization of the re-membering ministry may change. In some re-membering communities team members, in addition to using their gifts and talents, have begun to specialize in certain ministry roles.

If a community is dealing with a large number of re-membering Catholics it might be a good idea to have one or several team members in charge of locating and training companions. This could be done together with the parish catechumenate team when they locate and train sponsors. As people begin to explore the re-membering community the team may find that they are experiencing many newcomers. Several team members may get together to discuss and to form a plan to work with newcomers. Those team members involved in Scripture sharing may meet to work on Scripture together. Catechists may get together to share ideas or other team members may want to gather to plan the public relations and printed material coming from a re-membering community. As team members begin to specialize they are, in fact, assuming the full responsibility for the re-membering ministry.

In a maturing re-membering community this ministerial responsibility will begin to shift from the parish leadership and the re-membering community leaders to all the team members and to the parish itself.

Burnout

Since the re-membering ministry is an ongoing and intense ministry and since there is potentially a large number of re-membering Catholics, burnout may become a problem for a maturing team. There are several ways to prevent burnout. First of all, there should be enough team members so that each member can have some time off from team duties. The more team members that share the ministry, the lighter the individual's ministry work load. This will probably mean that a team will be searching for new members as the ministry grows. Each team member should have a clear understanding of the hours and time of their commitment to the re-membering ministry. There must be time for team prayer and social activities. The specialization mentioned above will also lighten the individual ministry responsibilities of team members. A team leader should always try to be sensitive to the burnout potential of the team.

Finally Joseph Favazza, in his book *The Order of Penitents,* calls for all the members of Christ's body to become reconcilers again.[4] A re-membering community team represents the parish and the whole Church in reconciling the inactive and alienated Catholics to the table of the Lord and to active discipleship as

---

[4]Joseph Favazza, *Order of Penitents: Historical Roots and Pastoral Future* (Collegeville: The Liturgical Press, 1988) 267.

apostles and witnesses for Jesus Christ. As ministers of reconciliation, the re-membering team has both an awesome and a joyful responsibility, but they will find that in ministering among the re-membering Catholics they too experience conversions and reconciliations. They will soon realize that working in the re-membering ministry brings them many companions in faith, many heart friends. To be a team member in this ministry is often its own reward.

Summary

The initial re-membering community team will be selected by the parish leadership and each team member should be a faith-filled person with abilities to share that faith. They should be joy-filled, gentle, non-judgmental, and have the ability to hold confidences. They should be able to build community and act as team players.

Ongoing team selection will vary according to the type and size of the parish. As the number of potential re-membering Catholics increases, the number of re-membering community team members will grow. It is possible to recruit to companionship and eventually to other ministry roles those people who have been penitents.

Whether a team is new or established it will be important to keep team formation a priority. Team formation should be ongoing and should include praying, playing, and preparing together. Team meetings are also important for a well organized team. As a re-membering community grows and matures, a team will have to deal with such issues as burnout, increasing size, and specializations within the ministry.

In forming a re-membering community team the important thing is to select key team members, do some planning, and then simply begin. Allow team formation to be molded somewhat by the needs of those seeking the companionship of the re-membering community.

3

THE MINISTRY ROLES
Gifts and Responsibilities

*There are different gifts but the same Spirit; there are different
ministries but the same Lord; there are different works but the
same God.*   1 Cor 12:4-6

BAPTISM GIVES EVERY BAPTIZED PERSON the rights and
responsibilities of bringing about the reign of God. Catholics
have come to realize that the call to ministry belongs to all the
baptized. Since Catholic Christian ministry is rooted in baptism,
the entire community is called by the Spirit to become the source
of this ministry. In recent years parishes have come to recognize this leadership of the community itself and to be comfortable with leaders chosen from the community. These leaders,
through the power of the Spirit, possess certain gifts or charisms
to be given for the good of the whole community. When community leaders recognize and use these charisms they are claim-
ing their baptismal heritage.

    The re-membering ministry relies heavily on the gifts or
charisms of the whole Christian community; therefore, it is important to find the specific ones that are necessary for the re-
membering ministry. It is also important that these gifts be recognized by both the individual possessing them and by the community itself since these gifts have been called forth by the Spirit
for service to the community.

There are special gifts or charisms that enable a person to fill the ministry roles of a re-membering team. Both the gifts and the ministry roles they empower are central to the re-membering ministry. There are the gifts that prepare one to fill the ministry role of community leader or a co-ordinator, gifts enabling one to be a companion in faith to a re-membering Catholic, charisms given a parish priest, gifts that empower a person to act as a spiritual guide, charisms in evangelizing or reaching out to the inactive and alienated, gifts that enable one to share the action of the Word in their everyday life, charisms for catechizing or teaching, hospitality or welcoming gifts, and gifts that manifest themselves in Christian service to others. No one of these gifts or charisms is greater than another for, in truth, each is important to complete the whole ministry of re-membering.

The re-membering ministry counts on all of these gifts working together. It then becomes unnecessary for any one individual to have all gifts. It is only essential to find a group whose members possess most of the gifts. When all ministers with their gifts are working together mutually, then a wonderful thing occurs. The ministry becomes more than the sum of the gifts. New energies, charisms, and power are released by the Spirit for the good of the whole community. The group of ministers becomes capable of things that they never thought possible.

The gifts and ministerial roles spoken of in this chapter will be the ideal toward which a new re-membering community will work. As we examine some of these gifts and ministerial roles, bear in mind that a new community will not need to have them all before beginning to work with the Church's alienated. Small re-membering communities should also note that one person may be able to fill more than one ministry role.

The Community Leader or Co-ordinator(s)

Every organization must have a strong leader(s) or co-ordinator(s) and this is especially true in a re-membering community where the emphasis is on ministry, journey of faith, and process of conversion and not on a specific written program. Whether a parish chooses one or several leaders as they form a re-membering team, they should select people with leadership gifts. Leaders will certainly need to have a talent for organization. They should be able to hold a vision of what the re-membering ministry is about and they ought to be able to sense what kinds of gifts and talents are important to fulfill that vision. Leaders will need to be able to recruit other parishioners with the required gifts and then to go on to enable them to carry out the mission of the re-membering ministry. But the most important gift that leaders will have is to be people of prayer who are in touch with their own reconciliation journeys.

We have discussed the importance of a re-membering minister who ministers among the inactive and alienated. In order to do this a leader, and eventually the whole re-membering team, must get in touch with their own feelings of alienation. They must acknowledge their penitential journey and experience the joy of reconciliation. A leader can get in touch with this journey toward reconciliation by spending a few days on a retreat specifically designed for this purpose. Such an opportunity is provided for people participating in a Re-Membering Church workshop presented by the North American Forum on the Catechumenate. It can also be done by journeying through the season of Lent in a manner similar to the journey in the order of penitents. It will happen on a continuing basis as a leader and the team participate as full members in the re-membering community. If a leader is a person of prayer, then touching the penitential thread of their faith journey will come naturally.

A leader is also an organizer! Let's face it, someone has to recruit and organize the team, plan the time of the sessions, reserve the meeting room, put the re-membering community on the parish calendar, organize the public announcements to let the parish know about the re-membering community, find the coffee pot, arrange to set up the chairs, and invite the inactive Catholics. Someone has to think of all the thousand and one things that go into running a group smoothly and then that leader must have the ability to enable the team to carry out these tasks. It is in good organization that ministry can flourish.

A leader is a visionary. He or she is someone who has a real feel for what it means to be an alienated and inactive Catholic, someone who knows what hurt is, who has consoled in the time of sorrow, who knows the joy of a reunion. A leader knows where the re-membering team and the re-membering Catholics are headed, someone who can see the joy of a reconciliation on the horizon.

A leader is a seeker of gifts, one who knows parishioners and is able to recognize the gifts of other people. A leader knows that they themselves will never have all the gifts necessary for a good re-membering ministry and is very comfortable seeking these gifts in other people, can recognize the parishioner who is gifted at greeting and working with people, knows how to find parishioners who can lead Scripture and who are willing to witness to the importance of Scripture in their lives. A leader recognizes social justice advocates, can select catechists and will seek people who are willing to share their faith journey with others.

A leader is a resource to the other team members. He or she should know where to locate books, people, and other media that will help the team carry out their ministry in re-membering. A leader needs skills for forming individuals into a team, and then the leader should have the further skills for enabling the team to carry out their ministry of re-membering.

A parish should choose the re-membering leader(s) or co-ordinator(s) wisely. A leader may be from the parish staff, one of the clergy, religious, or laity, but there should always be a co-leader from the parish community. Since the re-membering ministry is very much of the entire Church, the leadership of this ministry should be from the whole parish community.

The leader(s) or co-ordinator(s) will be the leavening of the re-membering community. They will be the ones that keep the community together and functioning smoothly. They will be the ones to help the community grow.

The Companion

Everyone in the re-membering ministry will experience companionship, but the fullest expression of companionship occurs when a specific person is chosen to be a companion to a re-membering Catholic. This ministering role of companion to a re-membering Catholic is another keystone of this ministry. A person who has been alienated and is considering a return to the active practice of their faith spends much time in meditation making life and faith choices, but when a decision has been made to search out truly the possibility of return, and when the returning Catholic turns to the parish community for support, then a companion is given to them. The companion will be a spiritual or ''bread'' friend who will journey at the side of this re-membering Catholic as he or she struggles with the healing, liberation, and forgiveness that is necessary for a joyful return. A companion is often the very place where a re-membering Catholic will find Jesus again.

A companion has many gifts to share. The companion needs to be a prayerful person of faith and one who is willing to share that faith with another. A companion must be a faith storyteller and a listener to another's faith story. A companion is a non-judgmental person who has the ability to listen to a re-membering Catholic with care but without passing judgment or trying to correct them. A re-membering Catholic needs to ask questions of their spiritual friend in complete confidence, knowing that the answers will be faith-filled from the life of their companion. A companion should be a sensitive Catholic who has seen the Holy in everyday life and one who can affirm this holiness.

Companions will pray together, sometimes in the middle of the parish community and sometimes quietly together. A companion is someone who can help their friend rediscover the joys of liturgy, private devotions, and personal prayer.

A companion who has similar views and personal qualities with the re-membering Catholic should be selected. Ideally, a companion to a re-membering Catholic is someone who has once been alienated and/or inactive. He or she is someone who has walked the returning journey and can understand the feelings and struggles of this journey. As the re-membering community grows, companions will usually be people who have been re-membering and reconciled Catholics within the re-membering community in the recent past.

A companion shares the return journey with the re-membering Catholic, but also is responsible for bringing the re-membering Catholic into the parish community. A companion will introduce a re-membering Catholic to the people, programs, and processes of the parish, will seek the gifts and talents of the re-membering Catholic and will help them become part of parish groups. The goal of working with a re-membering Catholic is to return them, as new creations in Jesus Christ, to the Eucharistic table, and to send them forth from the table as apostles and witnesses. It is the job of a companion to enable a re-membering Catholic to discover where they can contribute to the whole Church community, where they can be a disciple. A companion should be sensitive to a re-membering Catholic who has the talent for singing or who is able to greet people and make them feel welcomed or for one who shows ability to proclaim Scripture or who has artistic talents. A companion will be the enabler as this newly re-formed Catholic becomes an active member of the parish family.

While companions are an integral part of the re-membering community team, they often serve in the ministry role of companion without fulfilling any other team roles. The service of companionship to a re-membering Catholic is usually a full time ministry.

A companion is the heart of the re-membering community. It is in the companioning relationships that we find true heart friends and touch the love of God once again.

The Parish Priest

It is very important to include a parish priest as a member of the re-membering community team. It is not necessary, however, that this priest be one of the leaders or co-ordinators. The time commitment on the part of a parish priest will vary from parish to parish, but a parish priest brings to the re-membering ministry special gifts and talents as both an individual Catholic and as an ordained priest. It is most important to have a priest who is comfortable with his own penitential journey and who has accepted his own need for healing, liberation, and forgiveness. The re-membering ministry needs priests who can celebrate the sacrament of penance because they have experienced the sacrament of penance, who can forgive and heal because they have been forgiven and healed.

The priest working in the re-membering ministry should be a sensitive liturgist. This priest must come to know the re-membering Catholics well in order to be able to celebrate their return with them. In the ritual celebrations of the returning journey, the whole parish community will become involved if the priest truly is in touch with the meaning of the re-membering celebrations. If a priest involved in re-membering speaks of this ministry in his homilies, then the whole parish becomes aware of the work of the re-membering community. As a presider at the reconciling celebrations with re-membering Catholics, the parish priest truly portrays his traditional role as leader and presbyter of the re-membering Church.

In the re-membering ministry a priest will often be called upon to serve as a spiritual guide or a confessor for those re-membering Catholics. Gentleness and compassion are important gifts for this.

A priest may be asked to speak for the Church community. It is often important to people new in the re-membering process to be able to confront and to ask questions of someone whom they see as representative of the Church leadership. Their questions will need to be answered sensitively but with the full teachings of the Church. It is also sometimes important for re-membering Catholics to have a trusted confessor where they can literally unload some of their problems.

Finally, a parish priest must be comfortable bringing his own personal charisms to the re-membering ministry. If he is gentle or firm, humorous or quiet, talkative or shy, then these gifts need to be recognized. Perhaps a parish has a priest with a wonderful sense of hospitality or fiery belief in social justice. They will need to recognize and use these personal gifts. If a parish priest is a good liturgist or a good catechist the parish should count their blessings and encourage him. Remember, too, that the parish priest, like the other members of the re-membering community team, will not possess all the gifts necessary for the whole. Team members should never forget that the parish priest will also be on his own personal penitential journey as he too touches his need for healing, liberation, and forgiveness.

The parish priest is the spirit of the re-membering community. He is the leader of prayer and the guide to the Spirit. Hopefully, he will be both brother and friend.

Spiritual Guide

As re-membering Catholics begin to re-establish a relationship with God—Father, Jesus, and Spirit—it is not unusual for them to seek a spiritual advisor or guide. It is important that this guide has experience in healing, liberating, forgiving, and is one who can help find the way through the tangled path that leads to reconciliation. A spiritual guide will also often be used by team members as their faith grows and deepens, especially during Lent.

The ministry role of spiritual guide is an ancient one that has been in Church tradition since very early Christian times, and it is one that is being utilized today as our culture becomes increasingly aware of the value of spiritual counseling. A spiritual guide is important in the re-membering ministry as the need for healing, liberation, and spiritual growth becomes apparent.

Spiritual guides may be men or women, laity, religious, or priests. When a re-membering Catholic or a team member seeks a spiritual guide they should certainly seek a qualified person, one that has certain charisms and has some training for the ministry role of spiritual guide. In his book, *Soul Friend,* Kenneth Leech speaks of a qualified guide as a person possessed by the Holy Spirit and a person of learning, experience, and discernment.[1] A spiritual guide will be a prayerful person who can guide and support with both strength and gentleness. The parish leadership should be of assistance to re-membering Catholics and team alike in the selection of a qualified spiritual guide.

Spiritual advisors will be the guides or path finders of the re-membering community. They will lead the way to the Spirit for both re-membering Catholics and team members. They will be the friends of the soul.

The Evangelizer

A re-membering community can be the best organized process within the parish, but without those who go forth to seek the inactive and alienated Catholics and to share the good news with them the ministry would die.

Evangelizers in a re-membering community are the ones who make the parish and the surrounding community aware of the activities of the re-membering community by telling the story. They are the ones who seek out the inactive and alienated Catholics and extend to them the invitation to try the Catholic Church again. They are the ones who communicate the good news of the gospel to all.

---

[1]Kenneth Leech, *Soul Friend* (London: Sheldon Press, 1978) 88–89.

The very best evangelizers for a re-membering community can be, in fact, the whole parish family. In groups of Catholics the question is often asked, "Does anyone know someone who used to be a Catholic and no longer practices?" It is not often that there is a negative response. Everyone knows one or many friends who were at one time active Catholics and who, for one reason or another, are no longer active. Dean Hoge, in his book *Converts, Dropouts, Returnees,* tells us that about forty-two percent of initiated Catholics at some time during their life drop out of church attendance for two or more years.[2] Pollsters estimate that there are currently about fifteen million inactive Catholics. The possibility for re-membering Catholics is large and the best evangelizers to find these inactive and alienated Catholics are their neighbors and friends who are also the members of our parishes. It is from the mouths of friends and neighbors that the first proclamation of the gospel can be easily made as faith stories are shared.

Parishioners need to be encouraged to invite their inactive Catholic friends back to the parish family through the re-membering community. People who are considering a return to an active life in the Church usually re-connect first through storytelling with an individual person, second with a small group like a re-membering community, third with a parish family, and then finally, after much work and time, with the Church at large. This emphasizes the importance of a personal invitation by an active Catholic to a potential re-membering Catholic.

Evangelizers will seek potential re-membering Catholics among their friends and neighbors, but also in parish programs around family life events, among those recommended by parish leadership, and in places where the lonely and troubled may gather.

It then becomes obvious that if this large task is to be accomplished, the evangelizing ministers will truly need to be the whole parish. In the re-membering team, however, there will

[2]Hoge, *Converts,* 10.

be one or several team members with the special charisms for being evangelizers. It will be these team members along with the whole parish community that will be responsible for inviting the inactive Catholics to take another look at their Church.

Evangelizers are the heralds of good news. They are the welcoming smiles and they are the inviters. They are the ones who gently encourage the alienated and inactive Catholics to try again.

Scripture Sharer

In the journey of return, one area that becomes important for all re-membering Catholics is a new look at the Scriptures or the large faith story. In many cases the Hebrew and Christian Scriptures from their Catholic past were just something that was read in church with a priest or a sister interpreting their meaning. In some cases a re-membering Catholic will have had little to do with the Bible. In a new light, a re-membering community will read Scripture and discuss how this applies to their personal faith stories. This will usually be a new approach for the re-membering Catholic.

Parishioners with the gift of being able to read Scripture and relate it to their personal faith stories and then to share these revelations with others will be great assets to the re-membering community. A re-membering community will not be looking for Scripture scholars since interpretations of Scriptures can easily be found in books and parish libraries. Re-membering communities will seek to share Jesus and his message of love with one another through the written messages of the Scriptures as they witness to this message of the good news of the gospel in their daily lives. It often happens that on hearing the importance of the message in another person's life, the message will become clear and important in the life of the re-membering Catholic. This is why those people who witness to the gospel easily are important on a re-membering team. Hopefully, every member of a team will eventually become a Scripture sharer.

The Scripture sharers are the witnesses of the re-membering community. They are the ones who speak of God working in and through their lives. They are the ones that lead the way to the hope of reconciliation.

The Catechist

The ancient role of catechist also has an important place in the re-membering community because while a community could not exist without gospel witness, companioning, and prayer, it also cannot exist without making clear the correct teachings of the gospel and the Church.

A catechist in the re-membering community is the person responsible for referencing the gospel and Church teachings on the subject being discussed and for presenting these teachings in a clear and easily understood manner as they echo the good news. While the catechist is not necessarily a theologian, the catechist is someone who knows source material and can use that material to respond to questions from re-membering Catholics. In a re-membering community it is often found that re-membering Catholics will have many misconceptions of the teachings of their faith. Perhaps they formed their thoughts and opinions from the local media or from misinformed friends. Perhaps their last recollection of a teaching was from early childhood. In any case it is often necessary to clarify misconceptions with a clear and accurate presentation of gospel and Church teachings. In presenting these teachings a catechist should be careful not to change the teachings with personal opinions or feelings. They should, however, always show how gospel and Church values affects their lives.

The catechist is the truth of the re-membering community. He or she seeks to teach and reteach the traditions of the Church and gospel values, and seeks to bring about understanding through accurate presentation of Church teachings and sensitive emphasis on the gospel and its message.

The Hospitality Leader

Those involved in hospitality make anyone coming to a re-membering community feel welcome. A parishioner with the talent for easy conversation, a happy smile, and a friendly manner is the one for this role in the re-membering ministry. When a potential re-membering Catholic gets brave enough to come to the re-membering community they need to be welcomed with open arms and made to feel at home. Those involved in hospitality need to see that the entire team is focused on this new friend.

A hospitality person is comfortable with new people and has the ability to put anyone at ease. He or she really enjoys people and the fun things of life and has a certain talent for organizing the social activities of the re-membering community.

In true scriptural tradition, the "coffee pot" is on and, before the discussion is begun, the potential re-membering Catholics are welcomed and fed. Fed with coffee, tea, and "goodies" and fed with warmth and companionship. It is over coffee that lots of one-to-one ministry is done. It is over coffee that new friends are made and beginnings happen. All too often in ministry we underestimate the great importance of the "coffee pot" or hospitality ministry. We forget that all ministry must begin with welcoming.

Hospitality people are the joy and comfort of the re-membering community. Theirs is the sweetness and joy of welcome. Theirs is the beginning.

The Service Leader

Parishioners involved in social justice are great additions to a re-membering community. If a re-membering Catholic is truly to become an apostle and witness for Jesus Christ, then from the very first they must be made aware of the social gospel. A member of the re-membering community team with a flair for social justice can see that this happens.

A person involved in social justice must be aware of the neighborhood community and all its assets and problems. They need to know local organizations and the needs of these organizations. They should be aware of other national and global needs and how a re-membering community might help.

Each re-membering community should be involved in some way in the social justice issues of their neighborhood. As a Christian community, the re-membering community should be reaching out to bring the gospel to others in their neighborhood. The social justice leader on a team should lead the way.

Those involved in social justice are the prophets of the re-membering community. They are the ones that will call the community and its members to Christian action.

Ministry Roles: A Common Responsibility

Finally, be aware that the ministry roles of the re-membering community will be found in many people and not in just one or two. Know also that, with the possible exception of the ministry role of companion, some people may have the ability to fill more than one ministry role. In searching for team members to fill these ministry roles, recall that the re-membering ministry belongs, through the gift of the Spirit, to the whole Christian community.

Most people who have been involved in the re-membering ministry have come to reverence the working of the Holy Spirit. All alienated and inactive Catholics who are considering a return to the Church have already experienced a call by the Spirit. The return to the Church is strictly the work of the Spirit and it is the responsibility of a re-membering community team, in the name of the Church, to mediate repentence, conversion, and reconciliation.

Summary

Through the strength of the Spirit given for the good of the community, the re-membering community relies on the gifts or charisms of team members to empower the ministry roles that are essential in the re-membering ministry. The ministry roles are community leader(s) or co-ordinator(s), companion, parish priest, spiritual guide, evangelizer, Scripture sharer, catechist, hospitality and social justice leaders.

In smaller communities one person on the team may fill more than one ministry role, but the primary roles to begin with are leader, parish priest, Scripture sharer, and catechist. The other roles may be recruited after a re-membering community has begun.

It will be through the gifts of the Spirit and the talents of the team who fill the ministry roles that a re-membering community will be able to represent the Church in bringing about repentence, conversion, and reconciliation.

4

THE COMMUNITY
Structures and Celebrations

(Christ) has entrusted the message of reconciliation to us. This makes us ambassadors for Christ, God as it were appealing through us.   2 Cor 5:20

AFTER THE TEAM HAS BEEN SELECTED and formation has begun, it will be time to think about the structures and celebrations of a re-membering community. First, the team should agree on a name for their reconciling ministry and they also should list the purpose or goals and objectives of the ministry. Then, attention should be given to such things as how often and where the community will meet, what these meetings will look like, what will be discussed, and what kind of ritual moments will be celebrated. While respecting the fact that all re-membering communities will be slightly different, this chapter will look at some general thoughts on what such a community could look like in action.

Discussion Sessions
There is more to discussion than talk

Planning

The first and most important event to organize in a re-membering community is the regular sessions or meetings of the whole community. Each re-membering community should select a day, a time, and a place to gather the community to share Scripture, to discuss issues, and to pray together. Usually it is important to stick to the same day, time, and place so that the whole parish community can come to know exactly how to get in touch with the re-membering community.

A day and time should be selected that fits in with the parish calendar and one that is convenient for most of the parish community. In the beginning there may be only a few potential re-membering Catholics, but as parish hospitality and the re-membering community become known the numbers should increase. This will be especially true in larger, more transitory parishes. As a re-membering community matures and becomes larger it may become necessary either to include another day or add another meeting space. An ideal size for a group is from ten to twenty-five people and sessions should last from one and one-half to two hours. Scheduling the sessions on a regular basis is important. The yearly calendar of sessions will be discussed in the next section of this chapter.

A comfortable meeting room with homelike furniture that can accommodate about twenty-five people should be chosen, and this room should be equipped with hospitality needs. The community should never gather with the barrier of tables between them.

Some parishes have found that it is good for the re-membering community to gather at the same time as the inquiry or pre-catechumenate sessions of the RCIA. While it is always important to keep these two processes separate, meeting at the same time can help facilitate the pastoral care of both groups. Many times a parish finds that people come to one process when they really belong to the other. Parishes also discover that whole families often seek God together. The conversion process of one family member can make other members take a good look at their relationships with God, each other, and the Church; therefore, the initiation (children and adults) and re-membering processes are often intertwined.

Content

A re-membering community consists of a team including companions along with re-membering Catholics, and potential re-membering Catholics. Each team member should have committed themselves to the re-membering ministry for a specific time, but the re-membering and potential re-membering Catholics will come and go through the community as their faith journey warrants. There should always be space for the new person who has been called by the Spirit to enter the process and the team will come to realize that many people who arrive in the re-membering community will decide to leave before completing their journey of reconciliation. Their conversion journey will not be at a point where they can make a commitment. A necessary element in the re-membering ministry is openness and good hospitality for all.

A re-membering community session should always begin with hospitality. The room should be set up in a comfortable, friendly way. The coffee should be ready and name tags for everyone are always a good idea. Rather than identifying a whole team with special name tags, tags might specify the people that will lead that evening's session *(see* Chapter 2, the "blur"). Be sure that several of the team are designated as greeters, for it will be most important that, when a person arrives at the door of a re-membering community, someone is there to greet them. A potential re-membering Catholic should feel welcomed, but not overwhelmed or trapped. Hospitality time, during or after a session, will also be important.

The first formal part of each session should include an introduction of all those present and some easy way for them to begin to tell their personal story. This can be as simple as having everyone tell their name and where they are from. Sometimes other non-threatening questions that require longer answers may be used. It is important to remember that the whole community, team, and re-membering Catholics is included in this exercise and that no one is made to feel uncomfortable or obliged to answer.

The sharing of Scripture is another part of each session. Selections from the Sunday or other pertinent Scriptures should be read, followed by personal faith sharing. This is not the time for intellectualizing the Scriptures, it is only a time for sharing personal faith stories that arise from the Scripture stories. This sharing should be led by a team member, but team and re-membering Catholics alike contribute to the discussion. Scripture sharing can happen in large groups, small groups, or between companions. It may be done by verbal sharing, but other techniques such as art or journalizing may also be used.

Many parishes have found that Scripture is often very threatening to an alienated or inactive Catholic, so it would be wise to allow a newcomer the freedom to join the Scripture sharing part of the session when they feel that they are ready. While they are making that decision the team may want to provide an alternative for newcomers in another place separate from the regular gathering of the community.

This newcomers' gathering, led by a team member(s), should be the place for explaining the re-membering process and for beginning to surface the alienating issues that a potential re-membering Catholic is bringing to the group. It is possible for both a newcomers' group and the Scripture sharing of the community to happen at the same time but in different rooms, thus allowing the easy access to Scripture sharing when a newcomer feels ready. An alternative idea is to have the newcomers' gathering at a time before the beginning of a regular session.

Even though members of a re-membering community will have these special newcomers' gatherings, it will still be necessary for one of the community's leaders to interview each new person. This one-on-one contact enables the leaders to get to know each potential re-membering Catholic on a personal level. It also gives the new person the opportunity to ask questions and make statements of a more personal nature. This initial interview should take place as a potential re-membering Catholic joins the community.

However a parish deals with the issue of separate newcomers and Scripture sharing sessions, the entire group should be brought together to discuss issues. The issues to be discussed in a re-membering community always come from questions asked by the re-membering Catholics. There is never a preset agenda. As a team gains experience they will begin to identify questions that are always asked. Questions can be sought in special sessions of the re-membering community that are devoted to issue raising and they may also be discovered in the discussions of the newcomers' gatherings. Many times questions that lead to lengthy discussions surface during a regular session or meeting especially at Scripture sharing time. Teams will eventually be able to organize several months' discussion topics as long as they always leave time for the unexpected but important questions.

Other techniques for soliciting questions can be used. A question box where a person can leave a question is a good non-threatening way for a shy re-membering Catholic to ask their question. Questions asked of companions that would benefit the whole group should be considered. A special time during each meeting for questions from the floor also works well.

Prayer should be included in each session of a re-membering community, but care is to be given in the selection of the type of prayer. Re-membering and potential re-membering Catholics often have trouble with prayer. The re-membering community should gently lead these people back to a prayer life. An easy way to begin is with traditional memorized prayers, especially the Our Father. Later, simple prayers of petition can be added. A team should be most sensitive to the comfort of the re-membering Catholics when praying. They will want to be aware that a re-membering Catholic's prayer life can be tenuous at first but that it will grow, and as it grows re-membering Catholics may eventually ask to attend Mass with the rest of the members of the community.

There are a few other things to keep in mind. First, maintain a complete roster of the re-membering community even though it will need to be revised often. Secondly, be sure that the adult members of the family of a re-membering Catholic always feel welcomed at the discussion sessions. Third, don't wait until the re-membering community is perfectly organized before inviting the alienated and inactive! The community can begin with some minimal organization and then allow those who will come to help mold the completed form of the process.

Summary

Select a day, time, and place for the re-membering community to meet for discussion sessions. Keep the day, time, and place consistent.

Discussion sessions of a re-membering community should consist of:

Hospitality and Welcome
Introductions
Scripture Sharing & Newcomers Orientation
Issue Raising and Discussion
Question Answering
Simple Prayer

(*See* Appendix A for suggested meeting formats.)

Social Activities

Let them be called my friends

In addition to meeting for discussion sessions, a re-membering community will eventually want to plan social activities. These can be in addition to the regular discussion sessions or occasionally held in place of a discussion session.

These activities provide the opportunity for members of the re-membering community to get to know one another on a personal level. This personal friendship will be important when true faith sharing begins. Social time is also a good opportunity to include the entire family of a re-membering Catholic, since it is likely that the conversion process of this re-membering Catholic is affecting the entire family unit.

Service Activities

Learning the meaning of discipleship

Service to the parish and neighborhood community should also be part of the regular calendar of the re-membering community. Since true discipleship means ministry among these communities, it is always modeled in a re-membering community.

The easy time for service to begin is Christmas, since there are many parish and neighborhood needs evident at this time. Every community has its poor with the corresponding care required; in every community you will find the hungry, the thirsty, the imprisoned, the stranger, the naked, the ill. The re-membering community is concerned with healing, liberating, and forgiving in a bodily sense that is united with a spiritual sense.

Following Christmas the members of the re-membering community should continue their work among the needy of the parish and neighborhood communities.

The Yearly Calendar

Around the year in the Re-Membering Community

One of the first questions that will be asked by a team planning the yearly calendar in a re-membering community is, "How often shall we meet?" It is a tendency to think of the re-membering community in terms of a school year (September to May) just as we do many other parish programs, but re-membering is a process of conversion with a broader time frame than other programs.

Instead, as a team initially begins planning for the yearly re-membering calendar, they should think in terms of a liturgical year rather than a school year. The team ought to discuss the liturgical seasons and what the Church is saying and celebrating at these times. They will need to see how the regular meetings of the re-membering community can fit into all that is happening in the parish and universal Church during the year. Regular discussion sessions during the seasons of summer, fall, Advent, winter, Lent, Easter, and Pentecost would be the ideal.

The frequency of these regular meetings will vary from parish to parish, but it is important that the re-membering community be available at some part of every season. Bear in mind that the call to conversion and the process of continued conversion belongs to God within God's time frame. The re-membering community needs to be available to assist conversion journeys when they are needed.

Some parishes meet almost every week the year around and some meet once or twice a month. Some meet for a series of meetings during each liturgical season while others meet for a specific block of weeks several times a year. Being conscious of the conversion journeys of the re-membering Catholics, a parish should select a yearly calendar that fits into the life of the parish and one that can be handled by the re-membering community team.

Let's talk about the calendar of a re-membering community that respects the liturgical seasons.

The summer sessions are in a quiet, ordinary time and therefore are usually less intense than some other times of year. In the summer a community may want to hold discussion sessions only every few weeks. They may also want to meet for more social activities. They will want to cover simple subjects left from the previous year. They should operate on a low key, in tune with the lazy days of summer, but they need to be available at least part of every month.

As the momentum in people's lives increases during the fall, so will the activities of the re-membering community. As in their daily lives people think of new beginnings, this will be a time for meeting new potential re-membering Catholics. The community will want to schedule an ample block of discussion sessions at this time: at least every week for six or eight weeks. This is a good time to raise important questions, to plan dates for discussing the asked questions, and for getting to know one another.

In the Church, Advent is a quiet, expecting time and so too the re-membering community should slow its hectic pace of the fall to the quiet of Advent. This is a good season to devote meeting time to prayer, and for the whole community to seek to serve the neighborhood community. It is also a wonderful time for holiday social gatherings.

Winter sessions before Lent will again have a sense of new beginnings. There will probably be a resurgence of new members and new questions. If a parish is also dealing with the weather, they may be doing their best to have just several discussion sessions in this time. It is during the winter season that discernment is made concerning those who will be ready to celebrate their return in the renewed order of penitents.

Lent is by far the most intense and most important season for the re-membering community. All members of a re-membering community will celebrate this season in the best way they are able. Some of the re-membering Catholics will be ready to celebrate their return by becoming penitents in the renewed order of penitents. Some of the re-membering Catholics, especially those who have newly joined, will still be preparing for this return. Some team members will be involved with the penitents and some team members will be working with the new re-membering Catholics. All members will begin the season together with a special celebration on Ash Wednesday. All members will celebrate the end of the Lenten season on Holy Thursday as the penitents rejoice in their return to the Eucharistic table. It is not unusual for a re-membering community to participate actively in the celebration of the Triduum.

During Easter time the re-membering community will continue to celebrate the return of the re-membered Catholics. They will spend time along with the entire Church community in discernment of discipleship. The re-membering community team and companions will encourage the ministry discernment of the newly re-membered. This is also a time of commitment on the part of the team and a time for enlisting new team members. As in most seasons, this season of renewed commitment is a time for seeking and meeting potential re-membering Catholics.

In order to make this year-round ministry a possibility in a busy parish, the re-membering team should do several things. First of all they will want to be certain that they have enough team members to ensure ample time off for everyone. Secondly, a team will carefully plan discussion sessions and other meetings in each season. A re-membering community does not need to meet every week, but they do need to be available some of the time every season. Third, realizing the yearly commitment of the whole team, team leaders will be cautious that members do not become overburdened.

While the first concern in scheduling the meetings of a re-membering community will be the discussion sessions, care should be taken not to forget to include social activities and service projects in the yearly calendar.

Summary

A re-membering community must make themselves available the year around, but the scheduling of this should be in accordance with parish and team capacities. As they plan their yearly calendar, a team should consider the liturgical calendar instead of a school calendar. Careful planning will be necessary in order to meet the needs of re-membering Catholics and the energies of the team.

Ritual Moments

Celebrating our journey

While there are currently no prescribed rituals for the re-membering journey, a parish will quickly recognize those times when prayer and ritual seem appropriate. Some ritual moments that may be important are the beginning of the reconciling journey, the celebration of a companion relationship, recognition of commitment to the journey of return, and the most important of all, the reconciliation.

When a companion is given to a re-membering Catholic, the moment should be ritualized. This celebration should be with the whole re-membering community or, if appropriate, with the whole parish community. This ritual moment recognizes the companioned relationship between penitent and companion. It will probably also mark the time when a re-membering Catholic begins his or her journey of reconciliation in earnest. This moment should be celebrated in word, song, and prayer.

Other celebrations of beginnings and commitments can be planned as a re-membering community sees fit. Communities may find that it is important for them to mark other stages of the penitential journey of return, but it will always be essential that these celebrations of ritual moments happen within the parish community.

The most important celebration in a re-membering community will be the celebration of the reconciliation of the re-membering Catholic. While celebrations of individual and communal penance are appropriate to the journey of return, this celebration of return is expressed to its fullest in a renewed order of penitents during the season of Lent.

The Order of Penitents

The renewed order of penitents is a sacramental expression of healing, liberation, and forgiveness, and of conversion, repentance, and reconciliation. While this renewed and developing order bears none of the harshness of its older ancestor, it does retain some special marks of the earlier order. First of all, today's order of penitents is a transitional order much as the catechumenate is a transitional order. Honoring the journey of conversion, the order of penitents allows its members to move at their own pace from the fringes of the Church to a full, loving discipleship within the Church community. Secondly, this journey of return is not made alone but with the aid, support, and prayer of all the members in that Church community.

While this renewed order of penitents asks its members to grow in the way they look at sin, healing, and reconciliation, it has its very foundations in the early history of the Church, Vatican II and the revised Rite of Penance, and the 1983 Synod of Bishops: "Reconciliation and Penance in the Church's Mission." The re-membering ministry and the renewed order of penitents is also a response to parish experiences. Many parishes have found that alienated Catholics who are seeking a return are showing up in the parish's process of initiation, the RCIA, that honors conversion journeys and relies on the ministry of the whole Church community. At the same time many parishes have found that their parishioners are generally staying away from the traditional "Saturday afternoon" confessions.

Those people working in the re-membering ministry have discovered that what many re-membering Catholics seem to be saying is not that the sacrament of penance is no longer valid, but that the way we celebrate it today is not enough. Author James Dallen, in his book *The Reconciling Community,* says that history suggests that the major root of the current crisis in sacramental penance today is that the long process of conversion so normal to the earlier concept of the sacrament has given way today to a mere momentary ritual.[1]

It is certain that re-membering Catholics today feel the need for more: more time on the conversion journey, more companionship from the whole Church community, more prayer, and much more time to uncover and to act on life areas that are in need of healing, liberation, and forgiveness. They seem to feel that only when they have this additional pastoral care can they

---

[1]Dallen, *The Reconciling Community,* 253.

validly and joyfully celebrate reconciliation to a merciful, loving God and his community, the Church.

A renewed order of penitents is celebrated during the season of Lent and contains some of the elements of a re-membering ministry, but in a much more intense way. A re-membering community team begins to think about the order immediately after Christmas. This is a time of discernment on the part of the team and the re-membering Catholics as to who is ready to celebrate their return.

Generally speaking, re-membering Catholics are said to be ready to celebrate their return if they have come to some understanding concerning the areas of woundedness, captivity, and sin in their lives and have made some reconciling life decisions about them. Also, they need to have undergone some conversion back to Jesus Christ, have made a new commitment to the gospel, and are seeking to join the parish community in the fullest way. Often a re-membering Catholic seeking full reconciliation with God and community will have come to realize that the process of conversion and reconciliation is a life-long journey. Usually this decision to celebrate a return is made by the re-membering Catholic with the guidance of the team and/or a spiritual guide. When the decision is made for a re-membering Catholic to become a penitent in the renewed order of penitents, the first thing that is done is to have that person make an appointment with the priest of their choice before Lent begins. This priest may or may not have been the spiritual guide of the re-membering journey.

The penitent will tell his or her whole story to the priest and priest and penitent together will decide an appropriate Lenten discipline or penance that will help that penitent on their journey of reconciliation. The priest chosen by a penitent should be available for talks throughout the season of Lent since it may be important to have his help along this reconciling journey. Experience has taught that the Lenten journey often takes a penitent to spiritual places and paths not conceivable before Lent.

Once penitents have told their whole story they are ready to celebrate the beginning of their Lenten journey of return on Ash Wednesday by the celebration of the confession of God's mercy.

The Ash Wednesday celebration of the confession of God's mercy takes place at a liturgy scheduled for the whole parish. It is entirely appropriate that this be a Liturgy of the Word only. At this time the penitents with their companions will gather around the symbol of salvation, the cross, and the penitent will confess the loving mercy of God that has brought them to this wonderful time, and they will declare their intention of beginning a journey of return to the Eucharistic table. The penitent is then marked with the sign of salvation in ash. The rest of the penitent Church community will join the penitents as they too are marked with the ashen cross, the sign of mortality and victory.

During the season of Lent the penitents and companions will continue to meet regularly with some of the re-membering team members to share Scripture and faith stories. These sessions could take place on Sundays with penitents leaving from the parish assembly in much the same way as the catechumens. This group could also gather at another time that is convenient to the parish. The important thing is to gather often and to share the journey of reconciliation. At this special time it is appropriate to use methods of deepening prayer such as journalizing, guided imagery, and meditations.

During the weekly gatherings, prayer will become increasingly important. The small gathered community of the renewed order of penitents will use many prayer forms, selecting those that are valuable to their particular community. All communities will want to include prayers for healing, liberation, and forgiveness. These prayers could be said at the end of a gathering of the order or during the Sunday assembly of the whole parish community. These prayers should include specific prayers for individual penitents and the laying on of hands, the ritual gesture of the Church's prayer for healing and the calling of the Spirit.

While the order of penitents is gathering, in public and alone, the entire parish community should be praying for the penitents. Penitents should be included in the petition prayers of all Masses and in the individual intentions of parishioners and parish groups.

A penitent relies on this prayer of the community as they journey toward reconciliation and discipleship. Penitents also rely on the support of their companion, who will become a true heart friend during this time. They will need the loving support of the entire re-membering community and they will rely on the guidance and support of their confessor. It is only through the complete pastoral care of the entire community that a penitent will be able to arrive joyfully at the Eucharistic table on Holy Thursday.

Holy Thursday's joyful celebration begins with the ending of the Lenten season and the public reconciliation of the penitents. Penitents and companions come to the gathered parish community behind the symbol of their journey and salvation, the cross. The presider will ask each penitent if they are ready to complete their reconciliation with the Lord and with his community, the Church, by assuming their place at the table of apostles and witnesses. When penitents have affirmed their readiness, the presider calls the entire community to prayer. Reconciliation is completed with the extended hands of the community and the laying on of hands by the presider while he speaks the words of absolution. In some parishes the relationship between baptism and penance is illustrated by the washing of the ashes from the heads of the penitents at the baptismal font. When these actions have been completed, the presider and the reconciled penitents may reverence the altar as a sign of their reconciliation. The community will respond to this in applause and by the singing of the Gloria. The true sign of peace will be exchanged by all.

Reconciled penitents and their companions can be included in other aspects of the Holy Thursday liturgy. It is especially appropriate to include them in the washing of the feet. Parishes might want to have the reconciled penitents dress the altar in preparation for the Eucharistic feast. They will certainly want the reconciled penitents, their companions, and their families to receive the Eucharist first or in some special manner.

Reconciled penitents along with the entire re-membering community will join the whole reconciled Church community in the celebration of the rest of the Triduum. The re-membering community should be present at all celebrations of the Triduum. It is most appropriate for the reconciled penitents, as a sign of their new discipleship, to lead the re-membering community in service to the catechumens as they are welcomed to the parish and Church community. The re-membering community may do this by helping at the remaining Triduum liturgies and by providing the hospitality for the newly baptized.

The entire Church community is changed again by every celebration of the reconciliation of a re-membered Catholic, and by this reconciling act the Church community itself becomes renewed and made whole once more. Reconciliation is the mission of the whole Church community, but it is also its salvation.

Summary

There will be several times during the journey of reconciliation when a ritual moment will seem appropriate, but the most important ritual moment will be the celebration of the reconciliation. Although paths to reconciliation are as diverse as paths of alienation, the selection of a renewed order of penitents is the fullest expression of the reconciliation celebration.

Appendix A
SUGGESTED MEETING FORMATS

The First Meeting

First, prepare the room in a home-like atmosphere. Have coffee and tea available. Make sure there are name tags and that several people have been designated as greeters.

15 minutes	*Introduction* and simple statement about self. Examples:
	1. "Where do you live?"
	2. "What kind of work are you involved in?"
10 minutes	*Explanation* of the re-membering process including when, where, and how often the meetings are held.
10 minutes	*Questions* about re-membering from the newcomers.
10 minutes	*Coffee Break*
30 minutes	*Issue Raising*
	This should be in group(s) of no more than four. The group(s) should be provided with questions that would help surface questions. Examples:
	1. What you always wanted to know about the Catholic Church, but were afraid to ask.

2. Tell Catholic stories of present day or of your youth.

3. Create categories where questions usually occur and have groups discuss their life experience from each category. These could include such things as sacraments, liturgy, Scripture, morality, Church history.

4. List the three things you like most about the Catholic Church. List the three things you like the least about the Catholic Church. List three questions you need answers to about the Catholic Church.

Have small groups ready to present results.

15 minutes   *Groups Report Questions*

Write these questions in a place where everyone can see weekly that the questions are being answered.

This initial exercise may take more than one session. Issue raising sessions will probably be needed in the Presentation time several times a year.

Other Meetings

Prepare the room as for the first meeting. Always be sure someone is ready to greet any newcomers.

10 minutes   *Introduction* of the entire group. Use one non-threatening question that will help everyone get acquainted. Examples:

1. What is your favorite dessert?

2. Name one funny thing that happened to you this week.

These questions put people at ease and also help you get to know one another.

20 minutes	*Scripture Sharing/Newcomers Group*
	Groups will be meeting in separate rooms.
10 minutes	*Coffee Break*
	Everyone comes together again.
10 minutes	*Hot Seat*

One team member is designated to take quick simple questions from anyone in the community. These questions should require a short simple answer. It is acceptable for the person on the hot seat to say they need to look up an answer.

Questions that would require a longer answer would be postponed until a presentation time.

45 minutes	*Presentation*
5 minutes	*Prayer*

Different parts of the meeting time may vary from week to week, and some weeks parts will be left out all together. An example of this would be a time when a visiting professional has been asked to do the Presentation section. Most of the meeting time might be turned over to them.

Optional Meeting Format

Prepare the room as usual. Invite newcomers to come thirty minutes earlier than the rest of the community.

30 minutes	*Newcomer's Gathering*
	Explanation of Re-Membering.
	Surfacing Issues.
10 minutes	*Coffee and the Gathering of the Community*
10 minutes	*Introductions*
30 minutes	*Presentation*

10 minutes   *Hot Seat Questions*

  5 minutes   *Prayer*

30 minutes   *Scripture Sharing*

Newcomers may stay or elect to leave at this point.

Meetings can be altered to make a longer prayer time.

Appendix B
RESOURCES
Some books to get you started

Scripture Sharing

Hamma, Robert, ed. *A Catechumen's Lectionary*. New York: Paulist
  Press, 1988.
At Home With the Word. Chicago: Liturgy Training Publications.
Powell, Karen Hinman, and Joseph Stinwell. *Breaking Open the Word:
  Cycles A, B, C*. New York: Paulist Press, 1986–88.
Serendipity New Testament for Groups. New York: Paulist Press, 1988.
Sharing the Word. Washington: Paulist National Catholic Evangeliza-
  tion Association.
Any of the many Biblical Commentaries.

Catechesis

Bokenkotter, Thomas. *Essential Catholicism*. New York: Image Books,
  1985.
Catholic Up-Dates. Cincinnati: St. Anthony Messenger Press.
Chilson, Richard. *Catholic Christianity*. New York: Paulist Press, 1987.
Cunningham, Lawrence. *Faith Rediscovered: Coming Home to Catholicism*.
  New York: Paulist Press, 1987.
Foley, Leonard. *Believing in Jesus. A Popular Overview of the Faith*. St.
  Anthony Messenger Press, 1985.
Hellwig, Monika. *Understanding Catholicism*. New York: Paulist Press,
  1981.
Killgallon, J., M. O'Shauhnessy, and G. Weber. *Becoming A Catholic
  Even if You Happen to be One*. ACTA Foundation, 1980.

Kohmescher, Matthew. *Catholicism Today.* New York: Paulist Press, 1989.

Link, Mark. *The Catholic Vision: An Adult Guide to Faith.* Allen, Tex.: Tabor Press, 1988.

Marthaler, Bernard. *The Creed.* Mystic, Conn.: Twenty-Third Publications, 1987.

McBrien, Richard. *Catholicism.* San Francisco: Harper & Row, 1981.

Wilhelm, Anthony. *Christ Among Us.* San Francisco: Harper & Row.

Appendix C
BIBLIOGRAPHY
ON PENANCE

Brennan, Patrick. *Penance and Reconciliation*. Chicago: Thomas Moore Press, 1986.

Brennan, Patrick. *The Reconciling Parish*. Allen, Tex.: Tabor Press, 1990.

Conn, Walter. *Christian Conversion: A Developmental Interpretation of Autonomy and Surrender*. New York: Paulist Press, 1986.

Dallen, James. *The Reconciling Community: The Rite of Penance*. New York: Pueblo Publishers, 1986.

Donnelly, Doris. *Putting Forgiveness Into Practice*. Allen, Tex.: Argus, 1982.

Favazza, Joseph. *The Order of Penitents*. Collegeville: The Liturgical Press, 1988.

Fink, Peter, ed. *Alternative Futures for Worship. Vol. 4: Reconciliation*. Collegeville: The Liturgical Press, 1987.

Friday, Robert. *Adults Making Responsible Moral Decisions*. Washington: NCDD, 1986.

Gallen, John, and James Lopresti. "Penance in Crisis." *America* (Oct. 10, 1987).

Gula, Richard. *To Walk Together Again: The Sacrament of Reconciliation*. New York: Paulist Press, 1984.

Hamelin, Leonce. *Reconciliation in the Church*. Collegeville: The Liturgical Press, 1980.

Hellwig, Monika. *Sign of Reconciliation and Conversion*. Wilmington: Michael Glazier, 1982.

Henchol, Michael, ed. *Repentance and Reconciliation in the Church*. Collegeville: The Liturgical Press, 1987.

Hoge, Dean. *Converts, Dropouts, Returnees: A Study of Religious Change Among Catholics.* New York: Pilgrim Press, 1981.

Keifer, Ralph, and Frederick McManus, eds. *The Rite of Penance: Commentaries: Understanding the Document.* Vol. 1. Collegeville: The Liturgical Press, 1975.

Kennedy, Robert, ed. *Reconciliation: The Continuing Agenda.* Collegeville: The Liturgical Press, 1987.

Lopresti, James. *Penance: A Reform Proposal of the Rite.* Washington: Pastoral Press, 1987.

Mick, Laurence. *Penance: The Once and Future Sacrament.* Collegeville: The Liturgical Press, 1988.

Mitchell, Nathan, ed. T*he Rite of Penance: Commentaries: Background and Directions* Vol. 3. Collegeville: The Liturgical Press, 1978.

Nelson, C. Ellis. *Conscience: Theological and Psychological Perspectives.* New York: Paulist Press, 1973.

Neumann, Donald. *Holy Week in the Parish.* American Essays in Liturgy. Collegeville: The Liturgical Press, 1991.

O'Connell, Timothy. *Principles for a Catholic Morality.* New York: Harper & Row, 1978.

Orsy, Ladislas. *The Evolving Church and the Sacrament of Penance.* Danville, N.J.: Dimension Books, 1978.

Osiek, Carolyn. *Beyond Anger: On Being A Feminist in the Church.* New York: Paulist Press, 1986.

Palmer, Paul. *Sacraments and Forgiveness.* Westminster, Md.: Newman Press, 1959.

Poschmann, Bernard. *Penance and the Anointing of the Sick.* New York: Herder and Herder, 1964.

Rahner, Karl. *Theological Investigations.* Vol. 15. New York: Crossroad, 1982.

Savage, John S. *The Apathetic and Bored Church Member.* Oittsford, N.Y.: Lead Consultants, 1976.

Schoonenberg, Piet. *Man and Sin: A Theological View.* Notre Dame: University of Notre Dame Press, 1965.

Slattery, Joseph. "Restore the Ordo Paenitentium?—Some Historical Notes." *Living Light* 20 (1984).

Sottocornola, Franco. *A Look at the New Rite of Penance.* Washington: USCC, 1975.

Taylor, Michael, ed. *The Mystery of Sin and Forgiveness*. Staten Island, N.Y.: Alba House, 1971.

(Prepared by The North American Forum on the Catechumenate. Used with permission.)

BIBLIOGRAPHY

Dallen, James. *The Reconciling Community: The Rite of Penance.* New York: Pueblo Publishing Company, 1986.

Favazza, Joseph. *The Order of Penitents: Historical Roots and Pastoral Future.* Collegeville: The Liturgical Press, 1988.

Hoge, Dean. *Converts, Dropouts, Returnees: A Study of Religious Change Among Catholics.* New York: The Pilgrim Press, 1981.

Leech, Kenneth. *Soul Friend.* London: Sheldon Press, 1978.

Lopresti, James. *Penance: A Reform Proposal for the Rite.* Washington: The Pastoral Press, 1987.

DATE DUE